Noah's Ark

First published in 1999 by Franklin Watts
96 Leonard Street, London EC2A 4XD

Franklin Watts Australia
14 Mars Road
Lane Cove
NSW 2066

Series editor: Rachel Cooke
Art director: Robert Walster
Consultants: Reverend Richard Adfield;
Laurie Rosenberg and Marlena Schmool,
Board of Deputies of British Jews

A CIP catalogue record for this book
is available from the British Library.

ISBN 0 7496 3218 6

Dewey Classification 221

Printed in Hong Kong/China

Noah's Ark

Retold by Mary Auld

Illustrated by Diana Mayo

W

FRANKLIN WATTS

NEW YORK • LONDON • SYDNEY

Long, long ago, God looked down at the earth and the people He had given it to. He saw that the people had filled His creation with wickedness and evil, and His heart was filled with pain. He was sorry that He had ever made men and women.

But there was one man whom God still loved. His name was Noah. Noah was a good and honest man. He lived his life with God at his side. And he had three sons: Shem, Ham and Japheth.

Now God spoke to Noah: "I have
decided to destroy all people because
they have filled the earth with violence
and crime. You must make yourself an
ark of cypress wood, three decks deep,
with many rooms. Coat it inside and
out with pitch. The ark should be 300
cubits long, 50 cubits wide and 30
cubits high. There should be a window
in its roof and a door on its side.

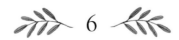

"I am going to bring a great flood and end all life on earth. Every living creature that breathes will die. But I shall make a promise - my covenant - to you: that you, your wife, your sons and their wives shall go into the ark with many animals. Inside, all shall stay safe from the Flood."

And Noah did just what God had told him to do.

Once Noah had built the ark, God spoke to him again. "You and your family must go into the ark. And you must collect together seven pairs of the animals I allow you to eat, seven males and their mates. And of every other kind of animal, you must take two, one male and one female. Of the birds that fly in the air, you must also take seven pairs, male and female. In this way, after the Flood, every kind of animal will once again be able to breed and spread across the earth. You must act now, for the rain will begin in seven days."

And Noah did everything that God told him.

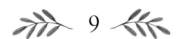

Noah was six hundred years old
when the Flood came. And on the day
the rain started, Noah and his sons,
Shem, Ham and Japheth, together
with their four wives, entered the ark.
And behind them came every creature
that has the breath of life.

Wild animals and farm animals, the birds of the air and the creatures that creep and crawl on the earth, all went into the ark, two by two, male and female, just as God had commanded. And when they were all safely inside, God shut them in.

Now the springs of the deep burst
apart and the floodgates of heaven
opened. For forty days and forty nights

it rained. The floodwaters rose and
lifted the ark high above the earth, and
it drifted out over the water.

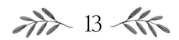

13

The floodwaters continued to swell and grew still higher, until even the tops of the mountains were deep under the water. And every living thing on earth died - all the birds of the air, all the animals that walked or wriggled upon the ground, and every single person. All life on earth was wiped out. Only Noah was left, and the others with him in the ark.

After forty days the rain stopped, but the floodwaters remained. Then God remembered Noah and the ark and sent a wind to dry up the water. The floodgates of heaven and the springs of the deep were closed. Slowly, the level of the water began to drop. Finally, the ark came to rest on the top of the mountains of Ararat.

After another forty days, Noah opened the window in the ark's roof and let out a raven, which flew to and fro until the waters on the earth had dried up.

Then Noah sent out a dove to see if
the ground was dry enough to walk
on. But the dove could find no dry
place to rest its foot, and returned to
the ark. So Noah put out his hand and
took the dove back into the ark.

Seven days later, Noah sent the dove out of the ark again. That very evening, the dove returned and in its beak it carried an olive leaf, freshly plucked from the tree! Now Noah knew that the waters were nearly gone. He waited seven more days and sent the dove out again. This time it did not return. It had made its home elsewhere.

Noah looked out of the ark and saw that the water had all but disappeared. Soon the earth was completely dry.

God spoke to Noah. "Come out of the ark," he said, "together with your wife, your sons and their wives. Bring out all the living creatures that are with you, the birds and the beasts. Let them spread out over the earth, and be fruitful and grow in number on every part of it."

So Noah came out, together with his wife, his sons and their wives. Every animal and every bird came out with him, too, one kind after another.

Noah built an altar to God on the mountainside, and he sacrificed burnt offerings on it. God smelt the sweet scent of the sacrifice and was pleased. He said to Himself, "I shall never again destroy the earth or the creatures that live upon it. For as long as the earth lasts, sowing and harvest, cold and heat, summer and winter, day and night will never cease."

Then God blessed Noah and his
family. "Be fruitful and increase, and
let your families fill the earth. All
living creatures, all the beasts of the
earth, the birds of the sky and the fish
of the sea shall be under your control
and care. I give them to you as your
food just as I gave you green plants.

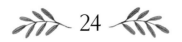

But I shall expect something in return
for this, and also for every human life.
Remember, I have made humans in
my image and whoever sheds the
blood of another person shall give up
their life as well. Now go out into the
world, let your families multiply and
fill the land with people once more."

Then God said, "I give you now a new covenant, which will stand for you and all your families to come, and every living thing on earth. This is my promise: never again shall I destroy all life with a flood.

"And as a sign of this covenant between me and you and all ages to come, I have set my rainbow in the clouds. Whenever clouds gather over the earth and the rainbow appears in the sky, I will remember my covenant and the waters shall not flood again."

So Noah, his family and all the animals and birds came down from the mountains and spread out through the land. And soon their children and their children's children filled the earth with life once more.

About this story

Noah's Ark is a retelling of part of Genesis, the first book of the Bible. The Bible is the name given to the collection of writings that are sacred, in different forms, to the Jewish and Christian religions. Genesis, which means 'beginning', is the first of the 39 books in the Hebrew Bible, Tanakh, or Christian Old Testament. Genesis is also part of the Torah, the most sacred text of the Jewish religion.

Who was Noah?

Noah was son of Lamech and a direct descendant of Adam, the first man, from whom he was separated by ten generations. In turn Noah's eldest son, Shem, was a direct ancestor of Abraham, the first of the Patriarchs, whom the Hebrew people saw as their founding father. The Jewish religion began amongst the Hebrews, so Abraham is also a founding father for Jews.

Much of the book of Genesis is concerned with setting out the links between the families of each generation. It was important for the Hebrews to be able to trace their ancestors right back to Adam. According to Genesis, people sometimes lived to very great ages - Noah lived to be 950 years old, his father Lamech 777 and his grandfather Methuselah to 969!

Surviving the Flood

Noah is a particularly important link in the Hebrew family tree because he survived one of the worst disasters to strike the human race, the Flood. No one knows for sure when and how the Flood took place but most people agree that, many thousands of years ago, a flood occurred in the Middle East region (see map) that was so great that people never forgot about it. Some archaeologists have suggested that the story recalls a time when the rivers Tigris and Euphrates flooded very badly. Another recent theory is

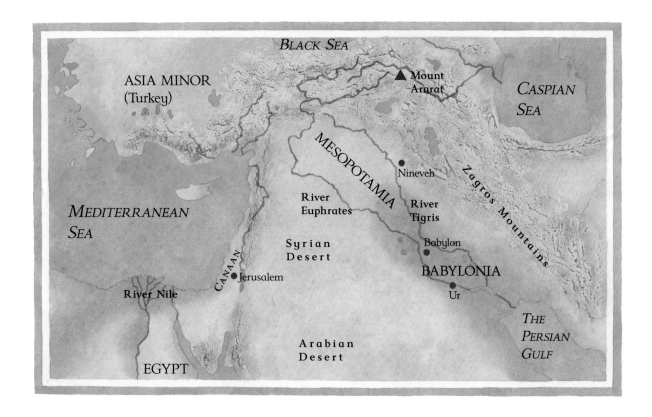

Map labels:
- BLACK SEA
- ASIA MINOR (Turkey)
- Mount Ararat
- CASPIAN SEA
- MESOPOTAMIA
- Nineveh
- Zagros Mountains
- River Euphrates
- River Tigris
- MEDITERRANEAN SEA
- Syrian Desert
- Babylon
- CANAAN
- Jerusalem
- BABYLONIA
- Ur
- River Nile
- Arabian Desert
- THE PERSIAN GULF
- EGYPT

that the Flood occurred when the Mediterranean Sea broke through to join the Black Sea, until then a much smaller inland lake.

The myth of the Flood

The Flood occurred long before people started to write. The first known written version of the story dates back about 4000 years, as part of a Babylonian myth. The Hebrews had strong links with Babylonia. Ur was said to be the birthplace of Abraham (who took his family to Canaan) and much later the Hebrews returned to Babylon as captives.

But the Flood story in Genesis differs from the Babylonian myth in a very important way. It sees the Flood from the viewpoint of a people who believed in one God, not many like the Babylonians. The Flood shows the power of God. He not only punishes the wicked, but also protects the good and ensures that life continues, even in the face of terrible disaster.

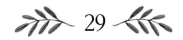

Useful words

Altar An altar is the special block or table, or sometimes just a pile of stones, on which a sacrifice is made. An altar is also the name of the table in some Christian churches on which Mass or Communion is celebrated.

Bless To bless someone is to wish him or her happiness and success in the future. A blessing from God is very powerful as it shows He loves you and is protecting you.

Covenant A covenant is an agreement or strong promise made between two people (or God and a person or people) where one person agrees to do something in return for the other person doing something else.

Cubits Cubits are a form of measurement people used to use like we use metres or feet. A cubit was the distance between the wrist and elbow of an adult man's arm - a little less than 0.5 metres, so the ark would have been about 140 metres long, 23 metres wide and 13.5 metres deep.

Cypress wood Cypress wood is the timber from the cypress tree, a type of evergreen pine tree that is common in the Middle East region.

Evil Evil is something very bad and wicked, which causes harm to other people and which God has no part of.

Honest Someone is honest who always tells the truth and does not hide things from others. An honest person is straightforward and trustworthy.

Mate A mate is one of a pair of animals, one male and one female, who have their young together.

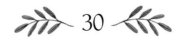 30

Pitch   Pitch is a black, shiny, sticky substance extracted from burnt wood or coal. It is waterproof so can be used to make a container watertight.

Sacrifice   A sacrifice is a gift or offering made to God to worship or give thanks to Him. In ancient times, Jewish people would sacrifice precious animals, such as a sheep, but animal sacrifice stopped after the destruction of the Temple about 2000 years ago. Today, a sacrifice can be something like using your precious time to pray to God or to help other people.

What do you think?

These are some questions about *Noah's Ark* to ask yourself and to talk about with other people.

What things do people do which you think are wicked and evil?

What do you think it means to say that Noah lived with God at his side?

What did you think about God's decision to flood the earth?

How do you think Noah, his family and the animals felt inside the ark?

How did you feel about the people and animals dying in the Flood?

What do you think Noah felt when the dove returned with the olive twig in its beak?

What has God given to Noah and his family and their descendants? Is it just food from plants and animals?

How important do you think it is to value and protect people's lives? Do you think it is ever right to kill someone?

How do you feel when you see a rainbow in the sky?

What does this story of Noah and the Flood show us about God?